Liturgy
Spiritual Formation

Carolyn Headley

Tutor in Liturgy and Spirituality, Wycliffe Hall, Oxford

GROVE BOOKS LIMITED
RIDLEY HALL RD CAMBRIDGE CB3 9HU

Contents

Part 1: Liturgy and Development 3

1.   Corporate Worship and Spiritual Formation 3

2.   Growth into Christian Maturity 7

Part 2: Formation Through Liturgy 11

3.   Formation by Encounter 12

4.   Formation by Learning the Faith 16

5.   Formation by Developing an Integrated Life 21

6.   Formation by Learning to Live in the Love of Christ 24

Acknowledgements

I would like to thank those who have acted as a catalyst to the work behind this booklet and those who have contributed to the practical suggestions offered. In particular I thank the students of Wycliffe Hall, the Readers in Willesden who looked at this topic for an in-service study day and the participants of a workshop at the GROW conference *Worship Beyond 2000*. I would also like to thank the GROW group for their encouragement and helpful suggestions in the writing of the booklet, especially Mark Earey, Michael Vasey, Jeremy Fletcher and Phillip Tovey. I am grateful to Mrs Corinne Smith for proof reading and commenting on the final draft.

'Liturgy is not a thing. It is the act of a people who gather with the Risen Lord to keep covenant with God—to hear God's word, to pray, to offer thanks and praise for the marvellous thing God has done for us in Jesus, and to leave with a mission. It is a moment in which we lift up the outward deeds and inner movements of our daily lives to allow them to be enlightened with a Gospel word and to be signed with a gesture of dying and rising. Liturgy is a verb, filled with people's celebrating and living.'

G Ostdiek OFM, *Catechesis for Liturgy* (The Pastoral Press, 1986) p 3.

The Cover Illustration is by Peter Ashton

First Impression October 1997
ISSN 0144-1728
ISBN 1 85174 356 1

Part 1
Liturgy and Development

A person who attends a service at church is in both an individual and a corporate relationship with God. There is a temptation to separate these two aspects of relationship. This is sometimes by concentration on personal piety and the privacy of our dealings with God. At other times the separation is by focusing on the corporate aspect and the activity of 'church' that we do together. Yet the biblical understanding is that there can be no separation. What we do together is integral to the whole of life and to all aspects of our discipleship as followers of Christ. Both alone and together we are in a relationship with the living God that is dynamic and life-changing. Through encounter with God we are formed, changed, and brought to greater Christian maturity.

In this time of liturgical change, with its inevitable focus on the corporate aspect of worship, there is an accompanying concern that our liturgy should foster, support and express the spiritual formation of the individual. Part 1 explores the way in which liturgy relates to our development and Christian maturity. Part 2 looks at how liturgy contributes to the process.

1
Corporate Worship and Spiritual Formation

Definition of Terms

The term 'spiritual formation' is used in this booklet to express the growth in Christian faith, character and practice that develops as Christ is formed in us (Gal 4.19). This growth is evident in every area of a believer's life. Formation is the process of learning, changing and growing into Christian maturity and the likeness of Christ. It is the work of God, through Christ and by the power of the Holy Spirit. It results from being alive to God in Christ Jesus (Rom 6.1-14), growing in understanding and experience of encounter with God, and deepening of our relationship with him.

The term 'corporate worship' is used to express the worshipping life of the church when its members meet together.[1] This needs to be understood in the wider context of the church transcending all physical boundaries of time and

---

1   See *Patterns for Worship* (Church House. 1995) p 193 for a variety of concepts expressed by the word 'worship.'

3

space. What happens in the life of a local gathering is but one tiny part of the life of Christ's body past, present and future, local and universal, temporal and eternal. However, for most Christians in the western world, the time that we meet together for corporate expression of relationship with God, and as part of our corporate encounter with God, will be Sunday services and, with less emphasis, weekday gatherings of various kinds. Corporate worship will refer to these times and what we do in them.

The term 'liturgy' is used to identify the set words, actions, and use of objects that we employ on such occasions.

The Relationship of the Individual to the Corporate Life of the Church

The whole history of God's dealings with humanity has been on a corporate as well as an individual basis. In the Old Testament the primary emphasis was on the corporate, with individual stories and actions being seen in the light of the wider relationship between God and his people.[2] There was a covenantal basis to the relationship, binding God and his people. Individual life was lived within the corporate covenantal relationship, with its laws and its blessings, its judgments and promises. It encompassed all of Israel and each individual within it.

In terms of worship we see an emphasis on the corporate in the temple worship and associated ritual. Although God's dwelling place was essentially in heaven, he nevertheless revealed himself on earth (as in Gen 28.12-13; 32.28-30; Ex 3.4-6; Ex 19.3-9). Then the tabernacle became the focal point for his presence (Lev 15:31; Ex 25.8-9; 40.34-38) and God was enthroned 'between the cherubim that were on the ark' in the midst of his people (1 Sam 4.4; 2 Sam 6.2; 2 Kings 19.15; Ps 99.1). In building the temple Solomon acknowledged with awe that God who dwells on high was also with his people (1 Kings 8.27-30; 2 Chron 2.5-6; 5.7-6.2; 6.41-7.3). The temple and Mount Zion were to become the 'permanent' location for the ark and the tabernacle, and so be God's dwelling place (1 Chron 28; Ps 84; Ps 132.7-8 and 13-14; Is 66.1-2).

The system for atonement of both individual and corporate sin emphasized the covenantal relationship, which was established and upheld by the blood of sacrifice. It was also later focused on the temple. Observance of the Sabbath, and attendance at feasts and festivals was an affair for the whole community in which Israel's special standing was celebrated (Ex 31.13-17), and God's guiding and provident hand was recognized (for example in the three major feasts of Passover, Pentecost, and Tabernacles).

Israel and Judah violated the covenantal relationship. Judgment for this was expressed by the corporate expulsion from Jerusalem and destruction of the temple. Restoration is expressed in the promise of a new covenant (as in Jer 31.31-34), return to Mount Zion with gladness, praise of God, and return of his glory (as in

---

2   O'Donovan helpfully traces the relationship of the individual to the community, although in the context of political theology and ethics rather than worship. 'The community is the aboriginal fact from beginning to end' O O'Donovan, *The Desire of Nations* (CUP, 1996) pp 73-81.

the vision of Ezekiel, Ez 39.17 to the end of the book, Isaiah, Micah and Jeremiah). From there God's glory would ultimately be shown throughout all the nations of the earth (Is 2.1-3), and God's Spirit would be outpoured (Joel).

In the New Testament the corporate side is still as strong as ever, with the establishing of the new covenant between God and his people through Christ. Many of the images for the church emphasize its corporate nature—for example Christ as the vine with us as the branches (John 15.5), a body with many members (Rom 12.4-5), and our being living stones being built into a spiritual house (1 Pet 2.5).

However, the New Testament also shows a new emphasis on the individual alongside the corporate identity we have in Christ. Through Christ and through his blood we are able to be in relationship with God as an individual, and to know the privilege of being eligible to come into his presence, and be recognized as a son of God and therefore co-heir of his kingdom.[3] We worship him in this context.

Corporate worship is evident in that this individual worship is within the wider context of the new Israel and the new covenant in Christ. We are a priestly people, a holy priesthood, offering spiritual sacrifices (1 Pet 2.4-9; Heb 13.15), in response to Christ's own sacrifice (Romans 12.1). The temple is Christ's body (John 2.20-22), and by the indwelling of his Spirit our own bodies (I Cor 3.16,17). In this new understanding of temple the living God still dwells in the midst of his people (2 Cor 6.16).

Jesus instituted a corporate act in Holy Communion. We come together to eat and drink in remembrance of his death until he comes again. Together we partake of his body and the blood of the new covenant (1 Cor 11.23-25). The importance of corporate worship is also evident in the frequent calls to come together. The church meets for the reading of Scripture, teaching, and prayer (Acts 2.42; 1 Tim 4.13; 1 Thess 5.27; Col 4.16), for praise of God (Acts 2.46-47), to break bread together (Acts 2.42,46; Acts 20.7; 1 Cor 10.16; 1 Cor 11.17-34), for mutual encouragement (Heb 10.25); for care of each other (Acts 2.44-45, 1 Cor 16.1-2), and to rejoice with those who rejoice and weep with those who weep (Rom 12.15).

This concept of the corporate nature of worship is vital for a correct understanding of both worship and spiritual formation. We need to live out our relationship with God both in times of solitude and in times of fellowship. This follows from an understanding of who we are before God individually and corporately.

Holding it Together

In this context it is interesting to note that the current emphasis on individualism in religion, which undermines the role of corporate worship, is not solely a product of the Enlightenment. It has its roots very much earlier.

Paul Bradshaw describes what he calls 'the divorce between liturgy and spirituality.'[4] Starting with the early church's desire to obey the scriptural injunction

---

3   'Son' is appropriate here, as it is important to realize the first century background, and the full significance of being granted 'sonship.'
4   P Bradshaw, *Two Ways of Praying* (SPCK, 1995).

to pray ceaselessly (1 Thess 5.17), he follows the struggle of how this was to be realized in practical terms. He demonstrates how various attempts at holding frequent corporate services during each day (Offices) led to the original function and aim being lost. The demands were unrealistic for most people, and other ways of praying developed.

Bradshaw observes that by the later Middle Ages individual, contemplative, and interior prayer began to be seen as spiritually superior to communal forms of the Offices.[5] He argues that this was strengthened by the Renaissance emphasis on the importance of the individual. Although this may be true as the beginning of a trend, there was still a desire by ordinary people for their devotion to be related to the communal worship of the church. Duffy[6] makes it clear that in the Middle Ages there was a great deal of lay commitment to the parish church, and to its liturgy, prayers and catechetical programme.[7]

The idea of the Reformation being wholly corrective of an ailing, or even moribund, corporate expression of faith therefore undervalues the evidence. Nevertheless the ideal was to renew corporate worship, and strengthen the link between it and personal reading and hearing of the scriptures.[8] It is somewhat ironic that the theology of individual salvation, and accompanying need to acknowledge personal sin, in humility and repentance, tended to reinforce a personal and individual devotion. So despite the original intention it can be argued that an individual pietism prevailed, at the expense of a truly biblical understanding of the covenantal and corporate relationship with God. The post-Reformation history of liturgy and spirituality continued to bear witness to the struggle between the two emphases of personal piety and a corporate sense of church, with what Bradshaw describes as the 'final separation' in the early 19th century.[9]

The two need to be held together, and helping church members to relate to God in both ways is necessary for a fuller and more meaningful use of liturgical form in our worship. Our liturgy needs to provide for an outworking of our individual relationship with God, in the context of our corporate relationship. It needs to start where we are and then take us, serve us, and accompany us in our personal relationship with God, as we walk together in the faith.

At its best liturgy is a vehicle that enables the people of God to make response to him. It helps us articulate what is there, encourages what could be there, and acts as a catalyst and an expression of worship. It opens us to the Holy Spirit, so he can engage with us together and individually as we stand in God's presence.

Given that corporate worship is integral to a person's relationship with God, and that liturgy should express and support this, the next question to be addressed is 'what is the growth and development to which we aspire?'

---

5   *ibid,* p 36.   **6**   E Duffy, *The Stripping of the Altars* (Yale, 1992).

7   *ibid,* Chap 4—commitment shown in giving and caring for the church; Chap 2—in learning the faith in a structured and thorough catechetical programme, which included learning the Lord's Prayer, ten commandments and Creed in the vernacular, and basic doctrine.

8   See 'Concerning the Service of the Church,' an essay at the front of the *Book of Common Prayer.*

9   *op cit,* pp 40-41, where Bradshaw gives a mixture of both social and religious reasons.

2
Growth into Christian Maturity

Growth in Christlikeness

The New Testament offers the goal of a life that is transformed into Christ's likeness. The new command is 'Love one another as I have loved you,' and the example is that of one who lays down his life for his friends (John 13.34 and 15.12-14). We too are called to love and self-giving after Christ's example—even to the cross. In living such a life of love we will be imitators of God and we will reveal the life of Jesus in our lives (Eph 5.1-2). This may mean a life of suffering (1 Peter 2.21) and a life which encompasses his death (2 Cor 4.5-12). We are also to follow in attitude (Phil 2.5) and in willingness to forgive others (Col 3.13). Whoever claims to live in Jesus must walk as he did (1 John 2.6).

So as Christ's disciples we aspire to bear the likeness of the man from heaven just as we have borne the likeness of earthly man (1 Cor 15.49). We hope for Christ to be formed in us—as was Paul's hope for the Galatians (Gal 4.19). We are to strive to be holy (1 Pet 1.15-16), and present our bodies as a living sacrifice to God, renewed in mind and honouring God (Rom 12.1-2; and 2 Cor 6.16-end). We are to reflect ever-increasing glory, which comes from the Lord, who is the Spirit (2 Cor 3.18). A holy life will show that the Spirit is at work in us (Gal 5.22). As Paul tells the Ephesians, we have been taught to put off our old self...to be made new in the attitude of our minds; and to put on the new self, created to be like God in true righteousness and holiness (Eph 4.22-24). The final transformation to Christ's likeness will be when Christ appears and we shall be like him (1 John 3.2-3).

This Christlikeness flows from a relationship of love, such as Christ himself showed in his relationship with the Father. Therefore Paul urges the Ephesians to be rooted and established in love that they may be 'filled to the measure of all the fullness of God' (Eph 3.14-19).

Despite the challenge to effect this Christlikeness by obedience and discipleship, it is clear that we need God's own love and power to be at work in us in order to make the transformation possible (Eph 3.14-19). As Christ promised he would he has come to his disciples (John 14.18). By his Holy Spirit God lives in us and makes his love complete in us (1 John 4.11-17). Being a temple of God's Spirit is not just to be a depository to hold it, but to be a way of God's presence and holiness continuing to be seen and known in the world (Eph 2.20-22; 1 Cor 3.1-6; 6.19).

Growth in Faith

We hear of Christ growing in wisdom and stature, and in favour with God and men in Luke 2.52. But the greatest concept of spiritual growth comes from Paul's epistles, where he passionately expresses his hope that those who come to faith will grow in it. These are sometimes known as his 'wish prayers,' and can be found in virtually every letter—usually just after the initial greeting.

If you go through the letters and put them all together, they form a remarkable picture of the growth for which Paul yearned in those who believe.[10] I have not put in references so that the full effect of this compilation is not interrupted.

Paul prays for those who believe...

that Christ: would dwell in their hearts and his power would fulfil in them every good purpose.

that God: would fill them with knowledge of his will; give spiritual wisdom and understanding; sanctify them through and through; encourage their hearts; give them a spirit of unity; strengthen them in every good deed and word; be glorified in them and them glorified in God; and keep them blameless at the coming of Christ.

that they: would be brought to perfection; be filled with the spirit of wisdom and revelation; have their hearts enlightened to know the hope to which they are called and the riches of God's grace; have strength in the inner being; know God better; be rooted and grounded in love; know the love of God; live a life worthy of their calling; bear fruit both in work and in knowledge; be strengthened with power; have endurance and patience; overflow with hope; be filled with joy and peace in believing; and joyfully give thanks to the Father.

In addition to the growth we should know during our life, there is also the hope of the ultimate maturity of faith in the eschatological hope of being changed, when we are brought into the fullness of the immortality and imperishability of resurrection from the dead (1 Cor 15.51-54). Paul personally looks forward to this in Phil 3.10 as he expresses his desire to become like Christ in his death, and so, somehow, to attain to the resurrection from the dead.

Growing into Wholeness

Many of the biblical concepts already mentioned can be understood by seeing wholeness as the ultimate goal of the Christian life. In the Old Testament, Israel's covenant relationship leads to *shalom*—and any departure from *shalom* through disobedience or sin, of individuals or the community, leads to dis-ease and a break in the harmony of perfect relationship with God, self, family, community and environment. This is demonstrated by the Deuteronomic formula with the promise of blessing for obedience, and warning of judgment for disobedience. The messianic promise is therefore also linked with the concept of perfect *shalom*, promising harmony at all levels of personal and community living.

The messianic hope is seen fulfilled in the New Testament emphasis on Jesus' healing ministry, especially when it is understood in the light of Luke 4.18-19 and 7.18-23. It demonstrates God's desire to heal all dis-ease, brokenness, sin, hopelessness and marginalization. Christ comes as the Prince of Peace whose king-

---

10 For a fuller treatment see D A Carson (ed) 'Prayer in Paul's Writings' in *Teach us to Pray* (Baker Book House and Paternoster Press. 1990 reprint 1994). esp pp 85-87.

dom is established within a new covenant, with a new law, and a new promise of blessing in wholeness, *shalom*, leading to eternal life.

Healing is brought about by God's power at work in Christ and supremely shown in Christ's atoning death and victorious resurrection and ascension. The church continues Christ's life, work and kingdom by the Holy Spirit being in its life and ministry.[11] Consequently we can also have the perspective of Christ's healing as part of our understanding of spiritual formation. We grow into wholeness, into eternal life.

This is important for liturgy in the need to see the church as a healing community, offering a dynamic corporate faith that reaches out in love and enfolds in love those who are in need of wholeness—which in effect is all of us. It therefore not only needs to have a proclamatory ministry but also a healing ministry. Formation includes accepting God's forgiveness, mercy, new life, reconciliation, restoration, and hope of eternity for oneself, and learning to minister it to others. Church members will share in that ministry by Christ's power at work in them as they use the full range of ministries and spiritual gifts. The priesthood of all believers is then at work, in sharing faith, hope and love in the midst of a broken and fragmented world.

Growth in Understanding

Growing into Christian maturity is therefore a rich concept, of growing in Christlikeness, faith, and wholeness. To enter into the process of change we need understanding, encouragement, and support. The teaching and preaching ministry of the church is therefore crucial to spiritual formation.

Through God's word we are drawn into knowledge about God, but also into a deepening personal relationship with the one who speaks it. One of the four elements in the greatest commandment is to love God with all our mind. Jesus uses the picture of the good soil which yields a crop for those who hear the word and understand it (Matt 13.23). Understanding is God's gift to us (1 John 5.20). It is one of Paul's hopes that the Colossians will be filled with knowledge of God's will through all spiritual wisdom and understanding (Col 1.9).

Growth into Christian maturity therefore includes growth in understanding. Much of this growing will be done in private reading and study, but the church gathering has a vital part to play. As Jesus 'opened the scriptures' to the disciples on the road to Emmaus (Luke 24.13-32), so the church is charged to be committed to read, teach and expound God's word. As we have already seen, the early church was diligent in passing on the apostle's teaching as they met together (Acts 2.42). Paul encouraged Timothy to be devoted to the ministry of the public reading of Scripture, to preaching and to teaching (1 Tim 4.13). He also commanded that his letters were to be read to the churches (eg Col 4.16 and 1 Thess 5.27).

Liturgy plays a crucial role in this growth of understanding, not only in explicit

---

11 Among the many good books on the Church's healing ministry are: E Lucas (ed), *Christian Healing* (Lynx, 1997) and M Maddocks, *The Christian Healing Ministry* (SPCK, 1981).

teaching and preaching, but through its wider teaching role, which is explored in more depth in Part 2.

Psychological Models of Growth

Psychological insights are also important, even if limited. Our humanity and our body with its senses, emotions, and character is the raw material with which we communicate with God and each other. A holistic view of our worship and our spirituality helps in understanding the process of formation. Two notable models for understanding growth in faith can be found in the work of educational psychologists such as Fowler in the United States, and in Jungian approaches such as personality typing using the Myers Briggs Type Indicator (MBTI™).

Fowler identifies stages in growth of faith.[12] There are six stages ending in a stage which only the likes of Mother Teresa and Martin Luther King have achieved or can achieve. It is generally an unsatisfactory model, both in its empirical basis with a research method that is somewhat inadequate, and in its theological basis which is highly selective. It is also primarily limited to the human life-scale without adequately seeing spiritual growth in eternal terms. However, it does go some way towards helping us to understand how we grow in our faith, and how churches can help their members to develop in their faith. It also suggests ways of identifying places where we get stuck in our development or get confused.

Personality typing recognises that we operate according to preferences.[13] It accounts for our individuality by demonstrating that we choose the way in which we make decisions, the things that interest us and absorb us, and the way we relate to people and the world around us. A personality type is indicated by the combination of the preferred functions that are identified (the MBTI™). Thus we have preferences for different ways of praying, different types of church, and different worship styles.[14] Personality will influence the way a church leader ministers in teaching style and managerial style, and the way a service is led. Personal growth towards maturity includes exploration and development of the aspects of prayer and worship that are not our first choice. In fact we are positively nurtured and enabled to grow by such exposure and experience.

These models challenge us to be aware that not all differences of practice and preference are theology-related. If we can see this positively then it may help us to cope with experiences we find difficult, and to be aware that we may be reacting on a human as much as a theological level. In turn this increases our ability to accept the validity of the preferences of others.

---

12 See J W Fowler, *Stages of Faith* (Harper and Row, 1981), J W Fowler, *Becoming Adult, Becoming Christian* (Harper and Row, 1984), J W Fowler, *Faith Development and Pastoral Care* (Fortress Press, 1987), J W Fowler, F Schweitzer, and K E Nipkow (ed), *Stages of Faith and Religious Development* (SCM, 1992).

13 Books on MBTI: I Briggs Myers, *Gifts Differing* (Consulting Psychologists Press, 1980), M Goldsmith and M Wharton, *Knowing Me—Knowing You* (SPCK, 1993).

14 C Bryant *Prayer and Different Types of People* (CAPT, 1983); B Duncan *Pray You Way* (DLT, 1993); M Goldsmith *Knowing Me—Knowing God* (SPCK 1994); R Innes, *Personality Indicators and the Spiritual Life* (Grove Spirituality Series No 57, 1996).

Part 2
Formation Through Liturgy

As already seen, we grow in Christian maturity in many ways, for in our humanity we will be developing in relationship with God, with all our heart and with all our soul and with all our mind and with all our strength, and in love and service of our neighbour. We will be growing in our understanding of God as we grow in knowledge about him as well as experience of him, and we will also be developing and growing in human psychological terms. Liturgy plays a crucial part in this process. The next question is 'how?' What is the learning process that occurs when we meet together that makes liturgy an integral part of spiritual formation?

An interesting exercise is to write down several things that you have learned, from any part of your life, and then work out *how* you learned them. For example you may think of learning to walk, tying up shoe laces, driving a car, changing a plug or the geography of the world. In examining the method you will find that you have learned through a multitude of ways. We learn by being instructed, and this can be by verbal, written, visual or multi-media presentation. We imitate the implicit example of others or an explicit demonstration of a skill (or avoid imitating when we observe bad example or have a bad experience). We learn by experiment, by trial and error. Our learning experience is guided by reward, praise and encouragement, or conversely by admonition and warning. We can get first-hand experience or visit the object of our study as in field trips. We may develop in our learning by practice, repetition or rehearsal. Sometimes we think things out for ourselves, sometimes we accept the knowledge and thinking of others on trust, and sometimes we imbibe knowledge from regular exposure to it.

When we think of formation through liturgy we must be careful to understand the same wide range of learning tools. We will learn through instruction and the reading and teaching of the word, but through so many other ways as well. In Part 2 we will examine just a few.

3
Formation by Encounter

Encounter with God

Learning by encounter is a common starting point—teacher to class, instructor to pupil, craftsman to apprentice. The gathered church in worship are the people of God who come into his presence through the Christ. We encounter God through word and sacrament, by his Holy Spirit. Any encounter with God is going to be formative, and part of God's larger work in our lives. As we engage with God during our time together we relate to him individually and together. This encounter will be life-changing, if it is real encounter.

As we encounter God we respond to him. In corporate acts of worship we do together that which we must also do on our own. We show our understanding of our need before our creator and redeemer, and our trust in the one who loves, forgives, and provides for us. We show our love for him in response to his greater love of us and sacrifice for us. We express our relationship with him, and our response to his activity in our lives and the life of the world. We demonstrate our life in a new covenant with God, in Christ. We live out our hope as we trust his promises. We respond in awe and gratitude in having access to his presence, undeservedly and not limited by time or geography. We open ourselves to his word and his Spirit, so that we can be taught and led by him as his people.

Being in dialogue with Almighty God, through Christ, by his Spirit, is a tremendous privilege. One great sadness for so many of us is the ability we have to shut off real encounter. We put up an inner screen in which we play the part and say the words, we hear the word read but it stays as an echo in our ears without cutting into our minds and heart, and somehow we manage to remain detached. It takes both an act of will, and the grace of God's Spirit to break through this detachment.

Preparation for worship can help in this, by prayer and time spent asking to receive God's word, giving him our attention and opening ourselves to him. The need to prepare is one that could do with a re-emphasis in our busy and rushed lives. The pace at which many of us live means that we fly into church with a hundred different things on our mind. That leaves little space for God's own personal activity. It is unrealistic to expect all our busyness will cease the moment we enter church—it takes time to quieten. It is not only important in terms of receiving from God, it is also important in terms of honouring him, and approaching him worthily.

Encounter with the Eternal Perspective

One of our church youngsters found it hard to distinguish between the word 'Pray' and 'Play,' so he used to refer to our once a week dawn prayer meeting as his Dad's 'Play Breakfast.' In a way he was not far wrong, for in that time of fellowship we found refreshment, and a sense of new life and new vision. (Not all of us every time, of course, but frequently it was so). As play can help to make sense and order out of daily experience, and can give rest, refreshment and joy, so can our worship.

Time with God, whether on our own or in fellowship with others, has the potential to change our perspective on life as we are reminded of the eternal perspective. It can renew our inner life as we are reminded of the infinite love and grace of God at work within us. It can lift us out of the difficulties of daily life as they are dwarfed by God's omniscience and omnipotence. It can let the light of God's presence flood into the dark places of pain and distress as we stand at the gateway of heaven. It can be a time of celebration and joy in our faith, and can give us space to rejoice in all God's blessings to us.

This blessing is both a present reality and a future hope. As Christians we have the promise of eternal life and life in the heavenly realms. We have inklings of what it can be like through our experience, and through revelation. Our worship forms a vital part in anticipating a whole life in God's presence eternally, our participation in the marriage feast of the Lamb, and being part of the hosts in heaven giving praise and worship to God. We acknowledge with Paul that 'now we see but a poor reflection as in a mirror; then we shall see face to face' (1 Cor 13.12). Our worship is so imperfect but it holds all the potential of eternity.

Our liturgy helps us to articulate this perspective, however inadequately. We listen to Scripture so that the word of God dwells in our hearts and brings knowledge of life that surpasses human wisdom. We open ourselves to the Spirit in prayer and silence, in use of his gifts and in receiving his blessing. We share in Communion which brings us together round the table in expectation of Christ making himself known to us in the breaking of bread, in anticipation of our Lord's return, and in anticipation of sharing in the heavenly banquet. Through the use of word, music, colour, artistry and ceremony, we try to express something of the worship of heaven, aware of the unseen reality of which we are part. Throughout our corporate worship we find infinity and eternity breaking into our human experience.

Encounter with the Community of Faith

As we meet together we engage with the story of our faith. Through the liturgy we both tell the story and participate in the story in word and action. 'Story' here does not hold any sense of make-believe; rather it is the account, the reciting and rehearsing of the collective knowledge, memory and experience of the Christian community. It is something of which we are part in our own time, and we in our turn will be part of the past story to future generations.

In the Old Testament, ritual related God's dealings with his people so that they remembered them. For example, the Passover instructions tell the story of what happened to God's people in Egypt and of its significance for all time (Ex 12.21-28); and Mordecai, in Esther, instituted the Feast of Purim to remember how God saved his people on another occasion (Esther 9.20-32).

Jesus gives us the commemoration of the Lord's Supper for the same reasons. 'Do this as oft as you shall drink it in remembrance of me.' It is a corporate activity through which the story is told of God's dealings with his people. It recounts the events and teaches us the significance, and in its performance we are both reminded of the truths and challenged to engage with them.

We have the cycle of the church's year with its focus on the life of Christ and its seasons and festivals which reinforce the Christian message. The lectionary provision, the reciting of psalms, and the regular and systematized reading of Scripture, all tell the story repeatedly in each generation.

Hearing the story of God's dealings with his people needs to be current as well as past. We could well re-emphasize the role of testimony and encouragement. God's present reality, power, love, action and involvement in our lives is part of the good news for today. It also helps equip us to talk to those outside the faith community if we have practice talking about God on home ground.

By meeting with each other regularly we also support one another.[16] We gather as the faith community, coming together to be renewed and helped to reorder and make sense of our daily life. In our times together in worship we have a period in which we recuperate and rest. It is not escape, but an opportunity to be fully at home with ourselves and our community, as part of the continuity of daily living.[17]

The liturgical framework provides a context of faith and an environment that gives meaning and encouragement to the faith community as a whole. From it we gain assurance, support and knowledge, individually and together, as we are caught up in its story, rhythm and cycle. So we learn it, are instructed and nurtured by it, and are formed by our participation in it.

---

16 The Cell Church Movement (and the 'New Way of Being Church') challenges the traditional pattern of meeting, and calls for a reverse of focus. Its emphasis is on seeing the 'church' not as the large gathering, but as people who meet primarily in small groups for their spiritual life, caring, nurture and fellowship. The large gathering is for celebration and the teaching and preaching ministry (a church of cells not a church with cells). See Simmonds et al, *A Future for House Groups?* (Grove Pastoral Series No 66, 1996).

17 Bruce Reed draws a parallel with oscillation in daily life. This is the way we alternate between "periods of autonomous activity and periods of...contact with sources of renewal" as described by psychologists—*a creative dis-engagement*. B Reed, *The Dynamics of Religion* (DLT, 1978).

---

18 For example the excellent course J Leach and M Earey, *At Your Service* (CPAS, 1997). The Alpha Course has a useful Bible study series on the church (not specifically about worship)—see the course manual, 1993 edition, pp 63-68 and Alpha Worship has an introductory teaching tape on worship.

19 For example *Emmaus: The Way of Faith* (Church House and Bible Society, 1996). Stage 3, Book 5. Some of the material may need adapting according to your understanding of 'sacrament' and local practice.

20 See M Earey, *Worship Audit* (Grove Worship Series No 133, 1995).

21 For helpful guidelines on planning services,see Patterns for Worship (Church House, 1995) pp 194-227, and pp 3-29 for specific planning of a Service of the Word and Communion.

22 For ideas on leading worship see C O Buchanan, *Leading Worship* (Grove Worship Series No 76) and on reading the Bible see *Patterns for Worship* pp 6-8, and M Vasey, *Reading the Bible at the Eucharist* (Grove Worship Series No 94).

14

Practical Suggestions: Formation by Encounter

Developing an Understanding of the Nature of Worship
- Home group series on the nature of worship For example: study of passages from Hebrews or Revelation; topics related to worship helping people to understand what it is, and think through ways of entering into it more fully;[18] studies on the meaning and content of services; general introduction to the relationship between worship and our life as Christians.[19]
- Worship audit to stimulate thought about the nature, purpose and form of worship.[20]
- Visits to other churches, followed by group discussion.

Before Meeting Together
- Congregational participation in service planning, including those who will be sharing in the leading or in music.[21]
- Training and preparation of ministers and others participating to prevent 'mechanical' or dismissive approach to liturgy, ensuring personal integrity and integration of the liturgical act with the whole life of the church and its members.[22]
- Providing a simple act of preparation for church members for use the night before or earlier in the day. For example a card can be devised with review of life, laying before God the things of concern, encouraging the taking of a few moments for quiet apart from the demands that clamour for attention.

When Meeting Together
- Encouraging quiet before a service, and corporate preparation. For example, the person doing intercessions that day going into the church five minutes before the service asking people to be quiet, reading a few verses of a psalm or other Scripture, making a simple prayer, and then inviting people to remain in quiet preparation until the service begins. Later arrivals then come into a quieter atmosphere and are encouraged to maintain it.
- Ensuring space and time for personal dialogue with God in use of silence or times of reflection for response. For example:
  - use of particular elements in liturgy such as the confession—giving time for reflection beforehand, and giving opportunity to identify one aspect of life that will be a focus in the coming week for prayer and discipline
  - allowing for reflection on the sermon—giving time to identify one particularly personal application that has arisen from hearing God's word.
  - use of responsive forms—to foster greater personal engagement.

After Meeting Together
- Theme of service, or sermon points given out—to encourage further reflection on content and on how God has spoken through the sermon or service.

4
Formation by Learning the Faith

Learning the Faith from Teaching

The most explicit teaching that takes place in the liturgical setting of corporate worship comes, of course, in the Ministry of the Word. Much work has been done recently in this area within many churches, both in the place given to it in liturgy,[23] and in the lectionary provision to guide it. *The Revised Common Lectionary* (and its C of E version[24]) encourages a more systematic and consecutive reading of Scripture, taking us away from the thematic approach of the *ASB*. This will stimulate us to re-emphasize expository preaching. How we expound the scriptures may vary according to local need and appropriate style. For example, we may take a didactic approach or something more along the lines of dialogue and engagement.[25] Ways to approach the use of the Bible and preaching in worship have been covered well elsewhere. It is sufficient here to underline the direct teaching role of liturgy in the Ministry of the Word, and to encourage a full use of the potential of this aspect of liturgy.

Learning the Faith on the Way

The church has a responsibility to provide for the nurture, care and teaching of all who come to Christ. Liturgy can have an important role in this by marking and affirming the process for all who set out on the way of faith. This is most obviously seen in the rites of initiation and the associated instruction. In current liturgical revision, in many main-line churches, this responsibility is being more fully examined, and a wide range of material is being produced.

The renewed emphasis is on developing a strategy for spiritual formation which is part of the life of the whole church community, and which is regularly and publicly supported and encouraged.[26] It is related to individual development but is programmed into the church life. The sort of rites envisaged aim to recognize and support the growth of faith in the individual.

For example, the Roman Catholic Church has produced the *Rite of Christian Initiation of Adults (RCIA)*.[27] This has a greater involvement of the whole church community, and an underlying programme that takes preparation and develop-

---

23 For example the Service of the Word in *Patterns for Worship* (Church House. 1995) pp 210f.
24 See *The Christian Year: Advent 1997 to Advent 1998* (Church House Publishing. 1997) and M Vasey and others. *Introducing the New Lectionary* (Grove Worship Series No 141. 1997).
25 See J Thomson. *Preaching as Dialogue* (Grove Pastoral Series No 68. 1996) and J Leach. *Responding to Preaching* (Grove Worship Series No 139. 1997).
26 This developmental approach goes back to the early church. in which a catechumenate (those preparing for baptism) was a common feature. See Tudge. *Initiating Adults* (Grove Worship Series No 102. 1988) which gives the background to the *RCIA* which more closely follows the early pattern than the proposals of *On the Way*.
27 *The Rite of Christian Initiation of Adults: Liturgical Edition* (Geoffrey Chapman. 1987).

ment very seriously. Similarly the more recent Church of England report *On the Way*[28] sets the scene for the current work on liturgical provision in the Church of England for initiation and associated rites.

The *On the Way* report calls for an approach which should include:

- Attempting to integrate personal formation, sacramental initiation, and incorporation into the life and mission of the church.
- Recovering of the significance of baptism for the ongoing life, calling and mission of the church.
- Emphasizing that the church has a vital role in the welcome and formation of new Christians.
- Realizing that coming to faith is a journey in which the enquirer needs the prayer and support of Christians.
- Taking seriously the need to respect the starting point of an enquirer and to learn from those whom God is leading to faith.
- Making clear that initiation and formation involve experience and reflection as well as instruction.
- Identifying four elements that should be part of Christian formation: worship with the church; growth in prayer; listening to the scriptures; service and witness in the community.
- Using progressive rites to help mark an individual's journey in faith and to enable the church to support them in prayer.[29]
- The report also suggests grounding discipleship in four basic texts: The Lord's Prayer, the Summary of the Law, the Beatitudes, and the Apostles' Creed.

In this way the spiritual formation of the individual is marked and affirmed in liturgy, and the process also contributes to further growth. Learning about worship is seen as one of the four key elements of Christian formation, giving opportunity for learning by example, participation, and involvement as well as instruction. The liturgy acts as a catalyst to the growing faith as individuals are drawn deeper into knowledge of God and into the life of the church.

Learning the Faith by Participation.

By praying to God and articulating our personal belief in the prayers of the church, we say 'yes,' 'that is what I want to say.' The received prayer becomes our prayer and part of our personal dialogue with God. The prayers, and other aspects of the liturgy, become more than mere tools; they form part of the dynamic of our encounter with God.

There is, however, another dynamic at work at the same time. Words and actions that we use to express belief can also inform, strengthen or affirm that belief. We not only express what we already know but are led into further knowledge, the knowledge of the community of faith. It is exposure to the scriptures,

---

28 GS Misc 444 *On the Way: Towards an integrated approach to Christian Initiation* (CHP. 1995). See Byworth. Read and Waller. *Joining God's Church* (Grove Worship Series No 134. 1995) for an introduction to the report.

29 *On the Way. op cit.* p 98.

doctrine and the experience of Christians through the ages. By involvement in the liturgy, both verbal and non-verbal, we learn. As we listen to, recite or sing God's word, and respond to it, we are enlightened and taught by it and led into the way of truth by the Spirit. As we use the prayers, creeds and confessions of the church we are drawn into greater doctrinal understanding. The creed may not only express what we already believe about God, but may also teach us more about him.

As we use symbols we reinforce the underlying truth they signify. For example, the bread and wine at Communion underline and reinforce the grace of God shown to us in Christ. They also facilitate response to that grace, and in so doing can become a means of grace to us themselves. So Article XXV reminds us that

'Sacraments ordained of Christ be not only badges or tokens of Christian men's profession, but rather they be certain sure witnesses, and effectual signs of grace, and God's good will towards us, by the which he doth work invisibly in us, and doth not only quicken, but also strengthen and confirm our faith in him.'[30]

This dynamic relationship between faith, doctrine and liturgy happens on both the individual level and on the community level. Liturgy is the meeting point of theology and practice, as is expressed in the ancient phrase *lex orandi, lex credendi*— the law of praying, the law of believing. In liturgy we find a two way process at work. Liturgy is informed by doctrine as we express the truths of the faith, and doctrine is also informed by worship of the living God as his people. Edward Foley says in *From Age to Age:*

'The Christian churches today acknowledge the ancient teaching that worship is the source and embodiment of our common belief. At the same time, worship has the power to shape and change our belief. More than official proclamation or systematic treatise, the liturgy announces who we are and who we are to become in Christ. Liturgy, therefore, is the bedrock upon which we build our theologies of God, church and salvation.'[31]

This teaching effect was one of Cranmer's prime concerns and explains why so much of the liturgy in the *Book of Common Prayer* is in the form of exhortations. It was later a concern to the Oxford Movement (in the 19th Century) and the subsequent Cambridge Camden Society and Ecclesiologists, who felt that some elements of the Christian faith were being inadequately expressed liturgically. For them there was need to restore the sense of the importance of the Eucharist and the symbolism and liturgy that expressed a high sacramental theology. It is something of which we are very aware in current liturgical revision, as we try to find agreed expression for agreed doctrinal understanding.

One of the great strengths of having a fixed liturgical form is this link with doctrine. It safeguards the doctrine by its incorporation in the worshipping heart of the church. It safeguards the worship by its agreed doctrinal basis, and it nurtures the worshippers in their faith. Conversely the provision of liturgy which

30 *Book of Common Prayer.*
31 E Foley. *From Age to Age* (Liturgy Training Publishers. 1991) p vii.

departs from Scripture and orthodoxy can also be learned, and can endanger the relationship with God. We must ask 'what is being taught?' and 'what is being imbibed unconsciously?'

Learning the Faith Through the Senses

The non-verbal aspects of liturgy can have as powerful a teaching effect as the words we use. Therefore they need to be addressed as we think about our formation. What are we learning from our environment, through our five senses?

Liturgy uses all of these to a greater or lesser extent. We have the use of sight in colour and symbols, ceremony, drama, art and architecture; hearing in use of word, music and bells; smell in using incense; touch in the sharing of the peace, laying on of hands and anointing; and taste with the physical intaking of bread and wine, to mention just a few. The ritual, whether celebratory or solemn, rich or simple, with music or silent, all contribute to the learning experience. The environment and the physical setting also teach.

For example, the building itself can speak volumes. The ground plan can remind us of the cross as in nave and transept style, or of an imperial court with all its grandeur as in basilica style. There can be elevated places to highlight importance, whether of the word in a grand and dominant pulpit, or of the sacrament in an elevated 'high-altar' or elaborate tabernacle or aumbry. A screen can speak of the separateness of the clergy and hierarchy, the holiness of the sanctuary or the holiness and otherness of God. As Mark Searle has put it:

'It is more than a sermon in stone: it is a multi-media communication of a version of the Christian gospel communicated in the shape of the building, its interior arrangements, its decoration and appointments, the kind of interaction it fosters or prohibits among the worshippers. Everything speaks, everything tells us who we are (for better or worse) and what our place is.'[32]

Those of us used to our buildings, and all other aspects of non-verbal liturgy, need to be careful that in our familiarity we do not forget what formation is going on through them.

Similarly we also model concepts in the way we do things. We model our understanding of the church in the way we gather. We model our understanding of ministry in the way priests, deacons, ministers and lay people function. Our body posture models our understanding of who we are before God and in relation to each other. We model our doctrine of God by how we treat each other, the strangers in our midst, and those in either need or plenty. We ourselves speak by our actions and therefore we teach. What are learning from one another? What formation of behaviour is happening in our church? What doctrine are we modelling?

In the multi-media and visual age in which we live, learning through many senses is expected. Are there ways in which we can positively enhance this?

---

32 Mark Searle, quoted in R Giles, *Re-Pitching the Tent* (Canterbury Press, 1996) p 59.

Practical Suggestions: Formation by Learning the Faith

Encouraging a Deeper Understanding of the Faith

- Short courses for church members on specific services, perhaps taking the main services and going through them to draw attention to the theology and doctrine, the richness of the concepts, and the potential for personal and corporate response to God.
- PCC day away[33]—especially at a time of revision and new services, but also in a time of stability when feelings and factions are less heightened—perhaps giving an introduction of biblical material; looking at the scope and purpose of alternative material; and rationale of use.
- Providing short liturgies that could be used at the start of confirmation classes, or at various stages in faith-building courses such as Emmaus and Alpha, to provide a way of supporting and encouraging participants.[34]
- Exploration of all-age worship with all-age learning.[35]
- Examination of the environment, and ways it can help in formation, or needs changing.

Before Meeting Together

- Instruction and support of worship leaders to understand theology. For example encouraging those in public ministry, especially the musicians, to attend local Christian education programmes.
- Looking at the doctrinal content of all aspects of the service as part of the team planning, including hymns and choruses.

When Meeting Together

- Drawing out links between liturgy and sermon, although care needs to be taken in how much this is done. It is important to maintain the main flow and response of liturgy.
- Using seasonal material to support teaching functions of calendar—perhaps using the same options for a whole season to enhance learning.

After Meeting Together

- Providing a week's programme of brief readings to aid reflection on the sermon topic, or in association with an ongoing teaching programme. These could also include some questions to provoke thought, and ideas for application and response.

---

33 See *Patterns for Worship* (Church House, 1995) p 195.
34 For example see *Emmaus: The Way of Faith* (Church House/Bible Society, 1996). Introduction pp 4-7, and for suggested texts see Stage 2: Nurture, Leaders Guide, pp 78-81.
35 See A Barton, *All-Age Worship* (Grove Worship Series No 126, 1993).

5

Formation by Developing an Integrated Life

Developing an Integrated Life of Worship

Robert Warren identifies the way in which a privatizing of religion has led to a compartmentalism that produces a false division between worship and daily life.[36] He quotes Richard Foster as saying

'many of us today live in a kind of inner apartheid. We segregate out a small corner of pious activities and then can make no sense out of the rest of our lives.'[37]

Our worship should be a whole-life expression of our relationship with God, and our liturgy in corporate worship should help us to ensure that it is. Through this integration formation takes place. This point is made by David Holeton when he says

'The Christian community assembled in prayer is engaged in "doing theology." What, and how, they pray is a primary theological and liturgical catechesis and provides the structure through which they come to know God for themselves, their community and the world in which they live. As such, the liturgy provides the basic resources to enable Christians to engage life in an integrated manner.'[38]

Jesus' summary of the law is to 'love the Lord your God with all your heart and with all your soul and with all your mind and with all your strength,' and to 'love your neighbour as yourself.' The relationship with God is to be expressed in whole-life response—our priorities and loves, our prayer and awareness of the eternal dimension of life, our use of intellect and thought, our physical activity, and the way we relate to those around us in the world.

The same principle is also inherent in our Lord's teaching on the kingdom of God. In the Sermon on the Mount he teaches the extreme importance of a faith that is lived out in practical actions. This point is taken up later in James' letter which specifically condemns any discrepancy between a claim to faith and the way in which the believer lives.

Paul says 'offer your bodies as living sacrifices, holy and pleasing to God— this is your spiritual act of worship' (Rom 12.1). In fact the whole of chapter 12 makes this point, and the subsequent chapters are full of the ethical implications of the gospel. Our life must speak of our faith, our calling, and God's power at work in us.

Liturgy can have a part to play in reinforcing this ethical side of faith.[39] Through

---

36 R Warren, *Building Missionary Congregations* (CHP, Board of Mission, 1995).
37 *Building Missionary Congregations*, p 13, quoting Richard Foster, *Prayer*, p 179.
38 D Holeton, 'The Formative Character of Liturgy' in Talley (ed), *A Kingdom of Priests* (Alcuin/ Grow Study 5) p 8.
39 See further Oliver O'Donovan, *Liturgy and Ethics* (Grove Ethics No 89, 1993).

liturgy ethical behaviour and Christian conduct can be supported and expressed. Forms for marriage, rites of reconciliation, and other pastoral liturgy can give voice and articulation to Christian principles. It can also provide expression for a personal ethic in teaching and preaching, and by helping us to come before God in review of life, confession, repentance, and recommitment.

Developing an Integrated Life of Prayer and Praise

The liturgy also helps in our formation by teaching us words and forms of praise and prayer that we can use day by day. The mechanism of repetition aids the learning process. The frequent repetition of sections of Scripture, psalms, canticles, and prayers become part of the working knowledge for a person's faith. They are used in spontaneous prayer or praise, in times of need and times of joy. They become a resource for the believer of material that is learned by heart for use from the heart. It becomes learning for life. It is the same learning principle as repeating the 'times table'—it becomes a tool and a piece of knowledge that is firmly anchored and stable, stored for use when necessary.

There is concern that the changing liturgical forms of our present age mean that the learning process is often not taking place. Serious questions are being asked about how are we to deal with this.[40] What will be repeated sufficiently to promote learning?

'The danger is that both the quality of some of our modern liturgical writing, and even the sheer variety of it, mean that generations are growing up that have no texts, new or old, in their memory to feed their souls.'[41]

One suggestion (by both the Liturgical Commission essays and the On the Way report) is to have core material that will be encouraged for frequent use and memorizing.[42] But what should constitute the core? On the Way suggests an absolute minimum of the Lord's Prayer, the Apostle's Creed, the Summary of the Law, and the Beatitudes (p 103).[43] The Liturgical Commission suggest a slightly wider basic fare including prayers from BCP and ASB services, collects, and some canticles (pp 93-94). Alongside these would be a further selection of important and established material. This collection is still under discussion, though a helpful collection along these lines is provided by An Anglican Companion.[44]

---

40 See James. Perham and Stancliffe 'Image. Memory and Text' pp 27-36. and M Vasey 'Promoting a Common Core' pp 81-101. both in M Perham (ed). The Renewal of Common Prayer (SPCK. 1993).

41 ibid. 'Image. Memory and Text' p 35.

42 ibid. 'Promoting a Common Core.' and On the Way. pp 102-103.

43 cf BCP. It is the duty of Godparents to ensure the Godchild learns the Creed. Lord's Prayer and 10 Commandments. and there is the direction that the Catechism is to be learned before coming to Confirmation. which includes these three and more.

44 Wilkinson and Cocksworth. An Anglican Companion (SPCK/CHP. 1996).

---

45 Celebrating Common Prayer, Pocket Version (Mowbray. 1994).

46 An Anglican Companion (Church House/SPCK. 1996).

Practical Suggestions: Developing an Integrated Life

Developing an Integrated Life

- Establishing the idea of rhythm of prayer in daily life, by a simple daily form of prayer or pattern of prayer used by the whole congregation—preferably in pocket-size form. (This, of course, is the purpose of the daily Offices, but for most people the whole Office is an unrealistic expectation if there is to be time for Bible study, reflection and intercession as well.)
  - The Liturgical Commission is developing something like this at present.
  - There is a pocket form of *Celebrating Common Prayer*.[45]
  - There are private publications such as *An Anglican Companion*.[46]
  - A home-produced form can take account of local needs.
- Use of, or development of, forms of service to make specific links between belief, discipleship and daily life—perhaps having a short series of daily forms of prayer with different emphases.
- Encouraging the learning of texts that will aid formation such as the Lord's Prayer, the Apostle's Creed, the Summary of the Law, and the Beatitudes (cf *On the Way*).
- Encouragement to use, and learn from, the Core material, or similar selection.

When Meeting Together

- Recognizing God at work in the daily life of church members. For example a series of short testimonies on different areas of work or home situations and how the believer relates to God in them. (This could be accompanied by a photo display).
- Opportunities for mutual exhortation, affirmation and encouragement.
- Positive value given to involvement in non-church activities, and through them to being a Christian in the world (but not of the world).
- Inspiration and encouragement to live with Christian values by looking at famous Christians and exemplars.
- Use of some material regularly to aid the learning process. This means balancing the need for creativity and flexibility with the need for learning by repetition.
- Regular use of responses and easily memorable short pieces of material to enable teaching effect of the liturgy.

After Meeting Together

- Enhance the mutual encouragement of learning by getting the whole congregation to
  - use the same prayer through the week on a daily basis, or
  - learn the same item for a season.
- Have a common seasonal greeting that the whole congregation uses whenever and wherever they meet.

6
Formation by Learning to Live in the Love of Christ

Living in the Love of Christ in Brokenness

The liturgy can bring Christ's transforming presence into places of need. It can enable people to feel tangibly in touch with God at the frontier of pain, violence, death, disaster, anxiety, hopelessness, and powerlessness.[47]

The primary liturgical focal point for brokenness is the Eucharist. In the last supper Jesus reveals the truth that he is broken so that our brokenness may be dealt with. In looking to Jesus, we see his self-giving love in life and death, his sacrifice for the world, and his forgiveness to sinners. And he met at table with those in need of his acceptance, love and forgiveness—the tax-collectors and sinners, and the disciples who so often let him down. And he taught about the heavenly banquet with an invitation to all.[48] So the eucharistic liturgy holds the pain of broken humanity, the promise of healing and the eschatological hope.

It is also important to hold the brokenness at other times and in other liturgy. Using psalms can be helpful, especially the lament psalms which groan with a desperate heart-cry to God, and the psalms of exile that resonate with many in our communities. For so many the daily experience is of being broken and without hope, or marginalized by what life has thrown at them, or just by being who they are or what they are. The liturgy needs to meet them where they are, and help them to express themselves in their relationship with God.

Work is continuing on new liturgy for healing rites and rites of reconciliation, and for funerals and those approaching death or actually dying. These mainly relate to individuals, but there is also the need to bring Christ's love and healing into communities. Here we may bring to mind the tragedies of Hillsborough or Dunblane, and the remembrance of past and continuing loss in war and conflict such as on Remembrance Sunday.

Sometimes we can do little more than hold the pain and brokenness before God, accompany those who are in need, and invite Christ to be with them in it. The transforming and renewing potential of encounter with God, eternity, and the community of faith (section 3 above), is not always realized at the time. By its prayer and liturgy, together with the actions and love of its people, the church shows forth Christ's love, and puts hope on the horizon. Those in need can be 'carried' and cared for. We know that by the incarnation, crucifixion, resurrection and ascension Christ has taken up broken humanity into the very God-head. As Robin Green says:

---

47 For fuller treatment of this idea see W Willimon, *Worship as Pastoral Care* (Abingdon, 1979).
48 For the Eucharist as a sign of being on the way, a repeatable sign of hope, a sign of spiritual recollection, a sign of presence of God, and an open invitation to an open feast, see J Moltman, *The Church in the Power of the Spirit* (SCM, 1977).

'The Christian believes that human life, however paralysed, however dark, however compromised, perverted, marginalized, or smashed up, has been taken up into the life of God.'[49]

Living in the Love of Christ in Ministry

If liturgy enables encounter with God, and encounter with God leads to changed lives, then changed lives must lead to service. The second part of the summary of the Law emphasizes the importance of loving our 'neighbour' (Matt 22.36-39). Christ's love, to which we aspire, is shown in self-giving. This must be encouraged by our worship which, as Peter Fink says, should be such that it

'stretches us to be for others—not for ourselves'…it takes us 'beyond self-fascination and beyond self-fulfilment into the mystery of God where the God-become-flesh is the centre and where human life, yours and mine, is transformed into the divine'[50]

Through intercession we look beyond our own needs to the needs of others. We reach out in assurance of God's greater love, and power to act. Scripture calls us to pray for each other and for the world.[51] The challenge for liturgy is to help us make good connections between intercessory prayer and an active concern for those for whom we pray. This will then more readily result in continued prayer, and altered lives, as we grow in love for those for whom we pray. Sometimes we find that this leads to actions as well as words.

We also show Christ's love by using the spiritual gifts when we meet together, to build one another up and be equipped for life and service (1 Cor 12-14; Eph 4.11-16; Rom 12.4-8). Learning to minister is part of our spiritual formation. We need to learn about the joy and wonder of discovering that God can use 'even me,' and know the experience of God's provision for the needs of others from beyond our own resources.

We have the supreme example in Jesus' teaching of his disciples, and their development as they trusted in God and experienced his power at work in them. Having taught them by word and explanation, having demonstrated ministry in his own words and deeds, Jesus then sent them out to try it for themselves. In Luke 10.1-24 we have the account of the sending out of the 70. When they returned they were exuberant and were falling over themselves to tell Jesus what had happened. He was likewise thrilled and rejoiced in prayer.

There needs to be a secure and safe place to learn by doing in the liturgy. This means giving opportunity for the practice and developing of gifts for ministry.

49 R Green. *Only Connect* (DLT. 1987) p 8. This helpful book is also on liturgy and pastoral care.

50 P Fink. 'Liturgy and Spirituality—a timely intersection' in E Bernstein CSJ(ed). *Liturgy and Spirituality in Context* (Liturgical Press. 1990) pp 51-52.

51 In intercession we are to pray for: those who need healing and forgiveness (James 5.13-16); our enemies and those who persecute us (Matt 5.44-45; Luke 6.28; 23.34); and those in authority (1 Tim 2.1-2). We are to pray for the Kingdom (Luke 18.1-8), for mission (Matt 9.35), and for one another's ministry. Paul urged the church to pray for him (Eph 6.19-20; Col 4.2-4; 1 Thess 5.25; 2 Thess 3.1), and the early church prayed for their needs and for power to preach and witness (Acts 4.23 ff).

This may be in reading, leading prayers, leading parts of the service, preaching, giving testimony, or in ministry teams, music ministry, or practical tasks.[52] There also needs to be a place for 'returning' and telling each other what God has done through us and in us. However, it must be recognized that this is not easy. It means accepting that something may not be done well. So the need for practical learning goes hand in hand with providing an environment where there is permission to fail. Failure is an important part of learning, providing it leads to further development of knowledge, experience or skill. If a failure is followed by refusal to learn from it, or by refusal to give further opportunity, or by condemnation or rejection because of it, then it is a destructive and negative experience.

There is a tension in liturgy between the desire to give the best possible to God, with as near perfection as we can humanly achieve, and acknowledgement that God also works through failure and mistakes. There can be no excuse for sloppiness or a casual approach to worship. However, the evidence of Scripture encourages us to be patient with failure, diligent in instruction, training and practice, and generous in co-operating with the God of second chances.

Of course, not everyone will have a calling and the appropriate gifts to be used in the public side of liturgy. However, the church that sees service and ministry as a natural outworking of worship and faith should release every member in their vocation as part of growth to Christian maturity. This cannot be by theoretical instruction alone.

Living in the Love of Christ in Mission

The Great Commission sends us out to go and make disciples of all nations. We are to be a people of witness and mission, and that should stem from our relationship with God, and therefore from our worship. In *Being Human, Being Church* Robert Warren says a missionary church will have

'a lived (hence earthed) spirituality—the church being, not just telling, the answers it is discovering. The result will be a group of people who know how to encounter God in their particular setting, and what sort of life appropriately expresses the good news of the gospel in that setting...'[53]

The heart of it remains where we started—the dynamic and life-changing relationship we have with the living God, through Christ, in the power of the Spirit. All that has been said about growing into Christian maturity, encountering God, learning our faith, living an integrated life, and showing Christ's love in prayer, ministry and service, will form us into a missionary church. Our corporate and individual lives will speak of God to the world around.[54] It is appropriate that the Communion ends with a dismissal which is a commission to live out our Christian calling, equipped and enabled by being in communion with God in Christ.

---

52 In the Church of England a Bishop's licence is required for regular exercise of preaching or for distribution of Communion.
53 R Warren, *Being Human, Being Church* (Marshall Pickering, 1995) p 152.
54 We read about this happening in the church in Thessalonica, where the message 'rang out' by their imitation of the Lord and their faith in God (1 Thess 1.6-8).

Practical Suggestions: Learning to Live in the Love of Christ

Learning to Live for Others
- Fostering concept of priesthood of all believers in the world, through preaching and teaching
- Teaching courses to prepare for different ministries, and support groups which encourage further learning and development of gifts.

Before Meeting Together
- Praying with all those who will be ministering, giving support and encouragement as they step out in faith, and rely on God's power and provision in ministry.
- Preparing for the worship with those ministering
  - Giving ample opportunity for practice
  - 'walking through' what will be done in a service
  - supporting by being aware of the courage and anxiety which most of us experience prior to ministering.

When Meeting Together
Drawing alongside pain and brokenness
- Welcome, acceptance, and involvement of those who are marginalized by society, from reception at the door, through the service and afterwards.
- Acknowledgement of hurting and brokenness—not just in intercessions; for example in the confession, Peace, prayer of humble access, invitation to communion, and fraction.

Ministry
- Making connections between intercessions and the reality of the situation.[55] For example:
  - using visual aids, or video of news reports eg Children's Newsround at a family service to help the young get a more global concept of intercession
  - photocopy of photographs or newspaper headlines onto OHP slides.
- Publishing of local needs for intercession each week to encourage continuing prayer.
- Creating ways of contributing concerns and issues for prayer. For example:
  - pieces of paper available at door of church
  - the intercessor standing in a known, designated place prior to a service
  Note that guidelines may be needed to prevent overlong intercessions.
- Time for personal reflection on intercessory needs with guidance.
- Creating a non-threatening environment in which to develop in ministry.
- Ministry to one another in prayer, conversation, laying on of hands.[56]

---

55 See M Vasey, *Intercessions in Worship* (Grove Worship Series No 77, 1981, 1988).
56 See C Headley, *Laying on of Hands in the Parish Healing Ministry* (Grove Worship Series No 104, 1988, 1992).

Mission
- Short testimonies about God using church members in a variety of different situations.
- Stronger emphasis on sending us out as in the Eucharist—perhaps using a prayer of commitment at the end of the service

After Meeting Together
- Use of published prayer rotas, which can be used at home.
- Giving immediate affirmation, encouragement, and recognition of those ministering. Giving remedial feed-back, further teaching and encouragement soon after ministry (but not at the time).
- Reviewing services with participants and church representatives to learn from good and bad practice.